EXPLORING WORLD CULTURES

Romania

Laura L. Sullivan

Cavendish
Square

New York

Published in 2020 by Cavendish Square Publishing, LLC
243 5th Avenue, Suite 136, New York, NY 10016

Copyright © 2020 by Cavendish Square Publishing, LLC

First Edition

Website: cavendishsq.com

This publication represents the opinions and views of the author based on his or her personal experience, knowledge, and
research. The information in this book serves as a general guide only. The author and publisher have used their best efforts
in preparing this book and disclaim liability rising directly or indirectly from the use and application of this book.

All websites were available and accurate when this book was sent to press.

Library of Congress Cataloging-in-Publication Data

Names: Sullivan, Laura L., 1974- author.
Title: Romania / Laura L. Sullivan.
Description: First edition. | New York : Cavendish Square, 2020. |
Series: Exploring world cultures | Includes index. | Audience: Grades 2-5. |
Identifiers: LCCN 2019017960 (print) | LCCN 2019018362 (ebook) | ISBN 9781502651631 (ebook) |
ISBN 9781502651624 (library bound) | ISBN 9781502651600 (pbk.) | ISBN 9781502651617 (6 pack)
Subjects: LCSH: Romania--Juvenile literature.
Classification: LCC DR205 (ebook) | LCC DR205 .S85 2020 (print) | DDC 949.8--dc23
LC record available at https://lccn.loc.gov/2019017960

Editor: Lauren Miller
Copy Editor: Nathan Heidelberger
Associate Art Director: Alan Sliwinski
Designer: Christina Shults
Production Coordinator: Karol Szymczuk
Photo Research: J8 Media

The photographs in this book are used by permission and through the courtesy of:
Cover ElePhotos/Shutterstock.com; p. 5 Walter Bibikow/AGE Fotostock/Getty Images; p. 6 Peter Hermes Furian/
Shutterstock.com; p. 7 Dziewul/Shutterstock.com; p. 8 Cristian Balate/Shutterstock.com; p. 9 Corbis Historical/Getty
Images; p. 10 Horacio Villalobos/Corbis/Getty Images; p. 11 Balate Dorin/Shutterstock.com; p. 12 Chris Ratcliffe/
Bloomberg/Getty Images; p. 13 Special View/Shutterstock.com; p. 14 Porojnicu Stelian/Shutterstock.com; p. 15 Cavan
Images/Getty Images; p. 16 MMCez/Shutterstock.com; p. 18 Ian Thraves/Alamy Stock Photo; p. 19 Daniel Mihaescu/AFP/
Getty Images; p. 20 Brenik/Shutterstock.com; p. 21 Osarbatoare/Wikimedia Commons/File:Dacian Sacred Fire ceremony
year 2013.jpg/CC BY SA 3.0; p. 22 David Forman/PhotoLibrary/Getty Images; p. 24 Florin1961/iStockphoto.com; p. 26 Dan
Potor/Shutterstock.com; p. 27 Gilbert Uzan/Gamma-Rapho/Getty Images; p. 28 Fanfo/Shutterstock.com; p. 29 Adriana
Sulugiuc/Shutterstock.com.

Printed in the United States of America

Contents

Introduction

Romania is a country in Europe. It is best known for a region called Transylvania. When people think of Transylvania, they often think of vampires. However, Romania has much more to offer than just scary stories. It is connected to the history and culture of many other European countries.

In the past, parts of Romania were ruled by the Ottoman Empire. Later, all of Romania became a free country. However, after World War II ended in 1945, the Soviet Union made Romania follow **communism**.

In 1989, there was a **revolution**, and Romania became a democracy. This means that the people choose the country's leaders.

Today, Romania is slowly growing. There are busy cities where citizens, called Romanians, live and work. People from other countries also visit these cities. There are sports to watch and restaurants with delicious foods to eat. Let's learn about life in this fascinating country!

The Romanian city of Bucharest has many old and some new buildings for its citizens and visitors to enjoy.

Romania has many neighbors. Ukraine lies to the north. Bulgaria lies to the south. Hungary is west of Romania, while Serbia is southwest. Moldova lies to the east. Romania also

Romania is bordered by several countries and the Black Sea.

borders the Black Sea on the southeast. The Danube River flows along Romania's southern border. The Danube is the second-longest river in Europe. It meets the Black Sea.

FACT!

Romania has many plateaus—high, flat, rocky areas that look like tables.

The Story of a Vampire

Transylvania is a region in central Romania. Author Bram Stoker's book takes place there. It is about a vampire named Dracula.

Romania has many hills and mountains. The Carpathian Mountains are in the center of the country. Moldoveanu Peak is the tallest. It is 8,346 feet (2,544 meters) high. It is colder in the mountains. The rest of the country has a temperate climate. This means that it is not too hot in the summer or too cold in the winter.

This famous rock formation is called the Sphinx.

In the first century CE, the Romans took control of what is now Romania. Many Romans moved there. Later, people from Turkey called the Ottomans took over. They ruled from the 1400s to the 1800s. Romania finally became independent in 1878. A **monarchy** was set up in 1881. It lasted until World War II.

Bran Castle was built in the 1300s.

FACT!

Romania means "citizen of Rome." It became the country's official name in 1862.

Michael I of Romania

After World War II, King Michael I (1921–2017) was forced to leave Romania. He returned when he was very old.

King Michael I was the last king of Romania.

During the war, King Michael was forced off the throne. Then, Romania's prime minister joined sides with Germany, Italy, and Japan. In 1944, King Michael took back his throne. He switched sides. Romania then helped England, France, the United States, and the Soviet Union win the war. However, the Soviet Union took over afterward. Romania was a communist country until a revolution happened in 1989. Today, it is a democracy.

Romania's government has three branches: executive, legislative, and judicial. The president, prime minister, and Council of Ministers make up the executive branch.

Viorica Dăncilă was the first female prime minister.

The president is elected by the people. The president chooses the prime minister. The prime minister runs the government. In 2019, the prime minister was Viorica Dăncilă. She was Romania's first female prime minister.

FACT!

A president's term is five years, and he or she can only be reelected once.

10

Parliament is the legislative branch of the government. There are two groups, the Chamber of Deputies and the Senate. They make the laws. Members of these groups serve four-year terms.

The Palace of Parliament is in Bucharest.

The judicial branch is made up of courts. There are courts throughout Romania. The highest court in the country is the High Court of Cassation and Justice.

Voting for Change

In order to change the Romanian **constitution**, the proposed change is voted on by all Romanian citizens.

The Economy

Romania is a member of the European Union (EU). This group of countries, or union, makes it easy for people, money, and goods to move between the different member countries.

This factory line shows cars from Automobile Dacia in Romania.

Romania's **economy** is one of the fastest-growing economies in the EU. Romania mostly trades with other countries in the EU, especially Italy and Germany.

FACT!

Automobile Dacia is Romania's biggest car company.

The Leu

Romanian money is called the leu. It means "lion." Soon, Romania plans to switch to the euro. That is the same money most other countries in the European Union use.

The leu is the Romanian currency.

Romanians have many different jobs. Some work in offices, banks, and restaurants. Others work in factories. They make things to sell to other countries, like cars, clothing, and electronics. Romanian farmers grow wheat, corn, barley, and potatoes. They also raise chickens and sheep.

More people are visiting Romania. They come to see the castles and the forests of Transylvania. They also come for skiing.

There are many wild, natural places in Romania. Close to half of the country is wild or partly wild land. The government protects these areas.

Pelicans and other birds live in the Danube Delta.

The place where the Danube River meets the Black Sea is called the Danube Delta. It is the biggest **marsh** in Europe. Birds like Dalmatian pelicans and rare ferruginous

The great white pelican is Romania's national bird.

Earth's Energy

Romania has started using **renewable** energy. Some comes from the ground. Another kind comes from water. All create power.

Hydroelectric dams turn flowing water into power.

ducks lay eggs there in the summer. There are fish like pike, carp, and catfish. Floating reeds and water lilies grow in the water.

Air and water pollution from factories is a problem in Romania. Also, parts of the Danube have been drained for farming. Today, Romania is trying to protect the environment. People are starting to use cleaner energy like hydroelectricity. This is power that comes from moving water.

The People Today

Over 21 million people live in Romania. Most are ethnically Romanian, or related to the Romans who lived there long ago. However, people with ancestors from other countries also live there.

These kids are wearing traditional Romanian clothes.

Many Hungarians, Germans, Ukrainians, and more call Romania home too.

FACT!

Many people have come from Nepal, China, and Vietnam to work in Romania.

The Roma make up about 3 percent of the official population. They are also called Romani. The Roma came from northern India a long time ago. Today, they live all over Europe. It is difficult to know how many Roma actually live in Romania because they are nomadic. This means that they often move from place to place. They usually stay in one area for a while and then move on.

Country Living

In most of Europe, more people live in cities than in the countryside. However, in Romania, more people live in the country than in big cities.

Lifestyle

Life in the countryside is different from life in the city. Romanians in the country are often more traditional. They tend to have large families with

Roma families often travel in wagons like this.

many relatives living in the same house. Extended families do not often live together in cities. Instead, families are small, with only one or two children.

The Romanian constitution protects women's rights. At home and at work, women have the

Almost 99 percent of adults in Romania know how to read.

same rights as men. For example, women must be paid the same as men to do the same work.

Romanian kids study in a classroom.

All children go to school. They have a year of preparatory school similar to kindergarten. Then, they must attend school through 10th grade. High school continues through 12th grade. Many students finish high school and go to college.

School Days and Nights

Some schools are so crowded that half the children have class in the morning and the rest go in the afternoon. Sometimes, the afternoon classes might not finish until 8:00 p.m.

Religion

Romania has no official religion. However, most Romanians are religious. In fact, Romania is one of the most religious countries in Europe. Christianity is the most common religion. About 81 percent are Eastern Orthodox. There are smaller groups of Roman Catholics and Protestants too.

The Metropolitan Cathedral is in Iași, Romania.

FACT!

Almost all of Romania's national holidays are religious as well. These include Easter, Pentecost, Ascension Day, and Christmas.

Religion in Government

Religion and the government are very connected in Romania. In fact, taxes are used to pay religious leaders.

There are about 73,000 Muslims in Romania. They mostly live in Northern Dobruja, on the Black Sea. Before World War II, there were also a lot of Jewish people living in Romania.

These Romanians gather to celebrate old religious traditions.

During the war, many were killed or forced to move. Today, there are only about 3,500 Jews in Romania.

A small number of Romanians do not believe in any god or follow any religion.

Language

Romanian is the official language of Romania. About 91 percent of the people speak it. Romanian is also spoken in Moldova, a country that borders Romania to the east. The Romanian language is used in

This Romanian sign has some letters with special markings below them.

schools, by the government, and for business.

FACT!

The Romanian alphabet is similar to English. However, there are letters with special markings, like Ä and Ï.

French in Romania

Many Romanians study French. It is considered an important language.

Other languages are also spoken in Romania. These include Hungarian, German, Russian, Ukrainian, and Turkish.

When Romania was communist, many of the different languages were not allowed. For example, the Roma were not allowed to speak their language, Romani. After Romania became democratic, people could speak their own languages again. Now, other languages are protected. For example, if someone who speaks another language has to go to court, he or she is helped by a person who speaks other languages.

Arts and Festivals

Romanian music includes everything from traditional folk to modern pop. Most folk music is played on the violin. Flutes or pipes can also be used, along with drums.

Lad's dances are just for men. Each dance differs from town to town.

Religious songs and special wedding songs are also performed with these instruments. Romania is known for its jazz and electronic music festivals.

FACT!

The National Easter Egg Festival shows off Romania's most beautiful Easter eggs.

There are folk dances to go along with folk music. These dances are performed in the countryside and during festivals. Often, the men of each community have a special dance. The dancing is sometimes a way to show off in front of women they want to marry.

The Sibiu National Theater Festival is a large, 10-day performing arts festival. People come from all over the world for classes, talks, and special performances.

Folk Arts

Traditional folk arts include sewing, weaving, wood carving, and pottery. They are still done all over Romania.

Soccer is the most popular sport in Romania. Both kids and adults love to play it. Thousands of people watch soccer clubs or the national soccer team play. The most popular soccer club is Steaua București. Handball is another very popular sport.

Handball is a favorite sport to watch and play.

Players pass a ball with their hands and try to get the ball in a goal. Some of the world's best handball players come from Romania.

FACT!

Most of Romania's Olympic wins have been in gymnastics.

A Traditional Game

Oină is a traditional Romanian game. It is a little bit like baseball. Players hit a ball with a bat and then run. However, they run in a different pattern than baseball players.

Other popular sports to play and watch are volleyball, basketball, and tennis. Rowing sports are also very common. Romania has won 19 Olympic gold medals for rowing and 10 gold medals for canoeing. People also come from around the world to ski in the Carpathian Mountains of Romania.

Nadia Comăneci is a famous Romanian gymnast who won many medals.

27

Food

One of the most common foods in Romania is *mămăligă* (muh-muh-LEE-guh). It is made from cornmeal. Sometimes it is soft, like porridge. It can

Mămăligă is a traditional Romanian food made from cornmeal.

also be made harder, like bread. It used to be a food for poor people. Today, most people enjoy it.

Ciorbă (CHOR-buh) soups are sour. There are different kinds, with different vegetables and meats. They get their sourness from lemon juice,

FACT!

Most Romanian cheese is made from sheep's milk.

28

Papanași (PAH-pah-nah-SEE) are special Romanian doughnuts. They are filled with soft cheese and topped with a ball of dough, fruit jelly, and sour cream.

Papanași are filled Romanian doughnuts.

vinegar, or sauerkraut juice. Sauerkraut is a sour cabbage dish.

Pork is the most popular meat. Many families that live in the country have their own pigs that they eat right before Christmas. They make many special pork dishes then. *Piftie* (pif-TEE-eh) is a dish of pig ears, feet, and tails. These ingredients are put into a gelatin and chilled.

Glossary

communism   A political and economic system where all property is shared by all the people.

constitution   A document that explains the laws of a country and the rights of the people who live there.

economy   The buying and selling of goods with money in a country.

marsh   A low area covered in water by a river or tides.

monarchy   A country ruled by a king or a queen.

renewable   Able to be used again and again.

revolution   The act of getting rid of a government through violence.

Find Out More

Books

Brinker, Spencer. *Romania*. Countries We Come From.
New York, NY: Bearport Publishing, 2018.

Finch, Jenny, ed. *The Vampire Book*. New York, NY:
DK Publishing, 2009.

Website

Geography for Kids – Romania

www.ducksters.com/geography/country.

php?country=Romania

Video

Lad's Dances in Romania

ich.unesco.org/en/RL/lads-dances-in-romania-01092

This video shows traditional Romanian dances.

Index

About the Author

Laura L. Sullivan is the author of more than forty fiction and nonfiction books for children, including the fantasies *Under the Green Hill* and *Guardian of the Green Hill*. She lives in Florida where she likes to bike, hike, kayak, hunt fossils, and practice Brazilian jiujitsu.